Breaking Through
Generational Cycles

No More Tears!

Breaking Through Generational Cycles

No More Tears!

Gisele Beatty

TATE PUBLISHING
AND ENTERPRISES, LLC

Published by Tate Publishing & Enterprises, LLC
127 E. Trade Center Terrace | Mustang, Oklahoma 73064 USA
1.888.361.9473 | www.tatepublishing.com

Tate Publishing is committed to excellence in the publishing industry. The company reflects the philosophy established by the founders, based on Psalm 68:11,
"The Lord gave the word and great was the company of those who published it."

Book design copyright © 2014 by Tate Publishing, LLC. All rights reserved.
Cover design by Joseph Emnace
Interior design by Honeylette Pino

Published in the United States of America

ISBN: 978-1-63063-070-6
Biography & Autobiography / General
14.01.10

Dedication

I dedicate this book to everyone all over the world who is dealing with a generational cycle and wants to see change. Open up your hearts and minds and let the healing begin.

Acknowledgments

I give honor and thanks to my lord and savior Jesus Christ.

To my husband Devin D. Beatty who was patient, loving, and understanding. My children, PJ (JedaVoice) and A'dana Patrice who love me and saw nothing but the best in me, and allowed me to share my love to my other children, Devin, Dajon, Bree, and Desmond.

To my mother Ernestine Carter who I give honor to for giving birth to me and being a big supporter in my life.

My oldest brother Timothy D. Bright who was always there for me and supported me as a best friend. My youngest brother Jeffrey Carter for being a great example of a good father to his sons in spite of his childhood. I'm very proud of him. My brother Alfred Carter, and Albert Carter thank you for your support. My other brother/cousin Marquel Bright, thank you. My sister/cousin Latisha Bright, a special thank you for your support.

Aunt Jewel and the late Willie Roseborough, a special thanks for always coming to the rescue every time I called. Cousin Tina Maria Doss Collins for being a big supporter and friend. Cousin Roxy and Ben Hunter for being big supporters.

My father's youngest brother Uncle John Carter and Aunt Chris for being supporters. My mother's oldest brother Uncle Raymond (Buddy) Bright for spending time with us and being a supporter. My cousin Wilbert and Bee Davis thank you for being supporters. My Uncle David Carter for being a supporter.

Thank you to all my family and friends.

Special thanks to my Great Aunt Iren John for giving me a better understanding of how life was in the old days. Special thanks to my late Uncle Callie James Carter for giving me an understanding of my father's roots.

Bishop Ron Gibson for believing and seeing God's favor in my life, thank you for your prayers and being a supporter.

A big thank you to Elder Roy and Cecelia Bennett who encourage me and saw the best in me.

Last but not least, thank you to my photographer Jonny and the entire staff at Photos Onsite Studio in the city of Moreno Valley, California. You all are the best.

Introductions

This book contains chapters of memorable short stories of incidents that have occurred in my life that will empower you to break the generational cycle of yesterday and began to see changes in your life today.

It gives me great joy to share a portion of my autobiography with element of biblical principles of my life, how I'm able through the grace of God to break the generational cycles of strong holds in my life which had me stuck in yesterday, confused about today with no since of tomorrow.

My heart was filled with many scar- tissues of painful memories which would bleed from time to time. Jesus healed and removed all the pain of my past, now I know what my purpose in life is, and my days are filled with promise.

I hope that as you read this book you to will begin to identify generational cycles that you may be experiencing in your life I ask that you take notes as I open up my life and share this journey with you how the pain was removed. And transforming into a new life of empowerment courage and peace now let the healing take place in your life and become free.

My desire is that everyone that reads this book will open their hearts and mind and let the healing began and sees how the power of forgiveness transforms their lives for a better life.

Contents

My Roots

On April 6, 1917, a little girl named Mae Mae was born to an unwed woman, my great-grandmother Lula. She was filled with joy to know that her beautiful baby girl, my grandmother, was born healthy. In those days, ladies who gave birth out of wedlock were talked about and rejected like outcasts. Lula, like most unwed mothers, felt unworthy and useless, even after dealing with the intense emotions of being an unwed mother—the shame, low self-esteem, bitterness, anger, hurt, and loneliness—and all the physiological and emotional changes she was going through, including fear of the unknown. This unwed mother hoped that one day she would meet a man who would love her and her little girl and share a happy life with her, hiding the scars in a broken heart.

Lula began to pull herself together, and as years went by, she began to forget what people were saying about her. She got out of the house and started to go into town. There she was introduced to a young man who took a lot of interest in her and her baby girl. As they began to date, feelings developed and grew into a strong love between them. The young man began to tell Lula how much he loved her and her little girl, Mae Mae. Although this boosted Lula's low self-esteem, it also set up the disappointment of false hope as this young man became the center of her real happiness. He asked my great-grandmother for her hand in marriage, and the two became one in holy matrimony.

My great-grandmother Lula was the happiest woman in Lower Peachtree, Alabama. Everything that she hoped for had come to pass—loving a man who loved her back and, with her child, starting a new and fresh life together… going against the odds… and never thinking about the man who had gotten her pregnant, moved away to New York, and started another family and left her with all the heaviness and pressures of life to deal with alone. This was all behind her. She was happy. Great-grandfather Joe wanted to start a family with Lula. At the time, life just couldn't get any better, and months later, Lula was with child again. That's when Joe dropped a bomb on her and said that when the baby was born he didn't want Mae Mae to live with them anymore; he said he only wanted the children that they were going to have together to be under the same roof.

So can you imagine what this expectant mother was going through? Her world had just turned upside down, and she didn't know what to do. Now she was faced with the biggest decision of her life, torn between her firstborn, little Mae Mae, and a man she loved and whose child she carried. As she asked the question, "What am I going to do?" all the past hurt, disappointment, sadness—everything that she had gone through—began to play back in her mind. So she decided to give her firstborn, my grandmother Mae Mae, to her mother as she tried to start a new life with Joe, the man she loved. Eventually, they had thirteen children, two stillborn.

Now my grandmother Mae Mae lived with her grandmother until she passed, and then my grandmother was given to her father's family, where she was raised by her aunt Betty. You must know how this little girl felt being around people she really didn't know and knowing that she had a mother but couldn't be with her and *now more* sisters and brothers that she couldn't grow up with. None of these stirring questions had answers. These issues were swept under the rug, you might say. What about Mae Mae? Who was she?

As years went by, my grandmother completed school, and she was the head of her class. Lula introduced her to a young man who also was the head of his class—a hardworking, entrepreneurial-minded young man, and the son of her stepfather

Joe's sister. This was Paul, who became my grandfather. And they were an ideal couple. They shared the same dreams and the same view of life together. Paul asked Mae Mae for her hand, and they were married.

She became pregnant and had a baby girl; they named her June. After a couple years, she became pregnant again. Mae Mae was sickly as she carried her children, so she gave her firstborn, June, to Paul's parents, and June stayed and lived with them indefinitely. Mae Mae and Paul had twelve children together, two stillborn. They did interact with their oldest daughter, but she did not live in the same house with her siblings.

My grandmother Mae Mae had no way of knowing that this pattern was part of a generational cycle: Years later, my aunt June gave her firstborn, Petey, to my grandparents to raise. My aunt April also gave her firstborn, Sara, to my grandparents to raise. And my mother, Summer, gave her firstborn, Chuck, to my aunt April to raise (she ended up raising three of her grandchildren). Later Chuck was taken to my grandparents to raise. My other two aunts, Misty and Raining, gave their firstborn children to my grandparents to raise, making a total of five. My youngest aunt, Windy, gave her firstborn to my mother to raise.

Somehow, no one sees how this is part of a generational cycle. In fact, all these firstborn children had to deal with rejection, abandonment, low self-esteem, and confusion, all rooting from my great-grandmother Lula, who had issues that were never dealt with. She carried Mae Mae in her womb with all this bitterness, anger, and hurt of having a man leave her and everyone in this small town talk about her. (When a woman is pregnant, she shares all those feelings and emotions with her unborn child.)

Then to have the baby, only to hand her over to her own mother—this set in motion a family history of deep scarring and a generational cycle of reacting to emotional turmoil within this bloodline. My great-grandfather Joe didn't want Mae Mae to be brought up with the rest of her siblings, and that created a scar that was embedded within her, a certainty that men really couldn't be trusted. Mae Mae didn't really have her biological parents to show her genuine love and acceptance and how to love. So she was doing things that she thought was right.

Mae Mae raised her girls to be independent and to never really trust a man to do anything for them. She taught them how to be self-sufficient, to work hard, and to make a nice living for themselves. This teaching she thought would shield her daughters from being rejected by men: *You really don't need a man to validate you—you know who you are.*

Mae Mae was a loving woman, but there was something piercing and bittersweet in her voice. It had a high pitch that could upset and break down a person, but with the same words, she could mend the damage almost without saying anything more. Each one of her daughters had the same pitch. They could chew you up and spit you out, but they could not hear themselves and this common thread to save their lives. They were part of a family who never seemed to see any good or positive, always focusing on the negative and haunted by the past, where the scars of thousands of cuts had been embedded within them.

My grandmother Mae Mae never felt the love from her mother, Lula. She always felt left out, and her siblings didn't know how to reach out because they had not grown up with her. Yes, they lived in the same town, but Mae Mae for her part also didn't really know how to give or to show love; she was still trying to understand love. From time to time, when her mother was sick, she would help with housework, or she would send a couple of her children to help Lula wash clothes, cook, and clean. She was desperate to feel love from a woman who had left her behind to start her new family. The hurt, always present, kept her from addressing the painful issues of shame, loneliness, anger, abandonment, rejection, and damaged self-esteem. All these unresolved feelings left scars not only in Mae Mae but also in her children, who also did not really know true love from one another or how to give it to their children.

Mae Mae loved her children, but because of the division in her early life, she had a division with her own children. In talking to them, she would speak blessings and curses out of the same mouth. She wanted her children to do well in life. She never told them she was proud of them, but she would tell them how disappointed she was with them, not seeing the good but always reminding them of the bad. Over time, this built a wall of separation within her immediate family.

Later, Lula passed away, and Mae Mae had never told her how she really felt and what effect their relationship had on her life. Mae Mae passed, and she never really told her brothers and sisters how she felt by not really being accepted by them. She loved her brothers and her sisters and her family, but she had scars from painful experiences that often played back in her mind. She would share the story with her children and grandchildren. These scars were never healed. Some of her children still talk about what happened years ago as if it just happened and are still bothered by it. You can see the anger build up in their faces when they think about what was told to them and what they actually saw growing up. These scars still affect them in some way today.

* * * * * *

Now my roots from my father's side. I don't really know about the history of my father's mother, Peggy, and his father, Juno. Although my grandmother got married at the age of thirteen and had thirteen children, Juno was a very abusive man who slapped and beat his wife. He would leave and be gone for months at a time. He was a lot older than my grandma, and he used that to his advantage. Now she was a beautiful, dark-skinned woman with a nice shape, and she was always well dressed. My grandfather was tall, high yellow, and nicely built, and he had a lot of women who wanted him. "Hey, good-looking, what you got going?" is what he used to say to the women.

When I spoke with Juno's younger brother, he stated that the Carter men in the family were "cursed with good looks"—tall, dark, handsome, and nicely built—and that the men were cheaters, always having more than one woman at a time. He also said that some of them were physically and mentally abusive. He said some of the women were cheaters as well and you would never see them without a man, and if a woman was married and had more than one child, it was possible that the children did not have the same father or her current husband might not be the father of any.

This was very interesting to me. I began to look around and saw that I also had children with different fathers. Wow—this was deep. At that time, I didn't know whether I thought he was just kidding around or was actually speaking the truth. I was told that my grandmother Peggy's children were not all fathered by my grandfather Juno and that some of her daughters had children with multiple baby daddies.

Indeed you must say that this is a generational cycle that has been passed down through the bloodline. Some get upset about it, some lie about it, some speak about it, and some don't want to know about it. When you can identify that this has happened more than once, more than twice, within the same family, it may not be a problem to you, but this is a problem that is identified, and changes need to be made for younger generations. It does no good to overlook it and say, "We're just family." It's time to make changes.

Now take a look. My grandma Peggy had different fathers for her children; her daughter did the same, and so did her granddaughter. This is a generational pattern within the same bloodline. This was not planned or a goal we set out to reach in our lives. The intent was to get married once, start a family, and live happily ever after. The stories of cheating and the abusive men and secret fathers were always kept quiet; no one ever wanted to address the issues at hand. Regardless, we see generational cycles over and over again as if it's okay. Not every male was abusive and not every woman strayed, but the pattern does exist within the family.

In this life, we may plan our lives one way, but they may take another direction—another way. And sometimes we may not understand why we go through so many turns in life. Keep reading, and some of your questions will be answered. My roots and your roots will help you better understand your tomorrow.

Raising Children

Both sides of my family were raised to go to church and believe in God, work hard, and dress nice.

In the days when my parents grew up, in a town where they had to work very hard picking cotton in the fields after going to school and trying to learn, they still had some hard chores to do. Picking cotton was hard on the hands and feet, and they dragged heavy sacks through the field trying to pick as much as they could before dark, still having to go to the well or the creek to get water to wash clothes or for drinking and cooking. Some had to milk cows, skin chickens, and work in the garden. Every day it was a hard job in comparison to today's living.

My grandparents on both sides had large families, and they did not have the intimate touch of showing love on a one-on-one basis. The only times they received attention were when they were sick or had gotten hurt. Other than that, it was just work hard, dress nice, and go to church—no hugs, no kisses, no "I love you." The kids had to just assume that they were loved, due to the fact that they had clothes, shoes, food, and a roof overhead—that's what they called love.

Now, in this day and time, children need more than just that. Children need strong communication and a meaningful touch from both parents or, if not, at least one parent needs to take special interest in the children. Be a strong support system for them; build up your children, boost their self-esteem, let them know how important they are to you, turn a lot of those frowns into smiles, reach out and hug your children, and tell them those three words—"I love you"—even when they think that they are too big or too old. Always remind them that you are never too small, too big, or too old to reach out and hug them and say, "I love you."

This plays a very important role in the mind of the child. When pressure comes to do wrong, that hug, that talk, that strong communication in "I love you" will play back, and it will make a child think twice about doing something wrong. A meaningful touch on the hand and a smile on the face will go a long way in the minds of children. Sometimes they will stray away, but they will not forget the times when Mom or Dad said, "I love you" and "You are somebody special. Yes, you can make it. You can do it. I am proud of what you did. You are going places. You are going to make it. I believe in you."

I am not saying that a child does not need discipline. It may not be enough just to pat them on the back and say, "I love you," expecting this to work for all children. Each child is different and may need a stronger or lighter approach to discipline tactics. "No, you cannot go to the movies," or "No, you cannot have this or that." If a child does not question you when you say yes, why should a child question you when you say no?

Certainly, some children are manipulators, some are destructive, some are liars, some are bookworms, and some are very smart. However, we must be able as parents to identify the different behaviors and patterns in our children, because they may have the same traits as the parents, like it or not. Because we know ourselves, we may be able to figure out what type of children they are and where their ways come from—their traits may be embedded within the heart of the parent. They may have the traits of the parent even more strongly in their personalities. Whether we like it or not, some of our children are a reflection of ourselves with ten on it.

Have you heard one of your girlfriends say, "My son acts just like his father"? I guess the question should be, "How were you as a child? Were you devious, goody-two-shoes, or destructive? Did you act wild, did you just like to hang out, or were you a bookworm who enjoyed school?" These are questions that should be asked before you even think about having a child. If you are deciding whether to have a child with any man, you should ask, "What type of child were you?"

When you build a child up, this builds our community up and builds our country up. When you tear a child down, this tears the community down and tears our country down. Children are our future. Make no mistake, this is a fact: children are our future.

Now we all know how to tear them down. We need to place emphasis on how to build them up; the street tears them down plenty. The streets can destroy their self-esteem. The street can destroy the yoke of positive possibilities. But we the parents have the ability to make our children dream of the possibilities through education, through technical schools, through the military, and through God-gifted talents (singing, acting, etcetera). These are things only God gives them the ability and urge to emulate, so we parents can always change a negative situation to a positive one by continuing to build up a child and not hurt him or her with words from our mouth.

Cultivate a mind-set of positive possibilities in your children, and you will see a positive result. You may not see it this year or the next, but you will see positive results that will give them hope and faith.

Generations
(Embedded Scar Tissue)

My grandma Mae Mae had a lot of dreams that she was hoping would come true and a lot of unanswered questions that she never asked. Grandma had a lot of disappointments, fears, tears, and painful memories of her childhood secrets embedded deep within her heart. It had all left scar tissue that would bleed from time to time—the pain of *what if* or *why haven't* or *do they* or *when will*, just a turmoil of memories, questions, dreams, and matters that were never spoken of.

Despite all this, Grandma Mae Mae was full of wisdom, knowledge, and contentment. Whatever situation she was in, she was content. She found happiness in her husband, children, and grandchildren. Let's not forget her church. Grandmamma would say, "If serving God is wrong, I don't want to be right." Yet she had these emotional scars that she would talk about, year after year, as if they had happened that day. And you could see the hurt on her face as she was telling a story of what had happened to her. This would upset her children and her grandchildren, as if it had happened to us.

Now Grandma Mae Mae has passed on, and some of her children and grandchildren still talk about how she was treated, getting upset as if it had just happened yesterday. They are holding onto the pain of the past of three generations. My great-uncles, great-aunties, and cousins still hold onto the pain of the past.

The truth is that the untold stories and hidden secrets that Great-Grandma Lula and Great-Granduncle Joe didn't tell to their children also caused a lot of pain and a lot of fears of the unknown truth. What memories brought tears of sadness to my Grandma Mae Mae—the hurt that she carried until the day she passed away? Her brothers and sisters will never know how my grandmother felt rejected by them or not really accepted by them. She was the firstborn of the same mother and yet felt an empty love in her heart, which she passed down to her children and grandchildren—not only her own children and grandchildren, but her siblings and their children and grandchildren.

We all are descended from one woman, Lula, but yet still there is a division within the family. The past is always talked about, and the walls keep getting higher. No one really tells my great-aunts or great-uncles how the past had really affected them in some way with the feeling of "not being good enough." Now families will come together if there is a death, sometimes a family reunion. Yes, we are always happy to see old loved ones, but that only lasts for a day or two before everyone is haunted again by the past.

Now there were some happy times; however, that is not the focal point. We always talk about the negative and reenact it as if it has just happened. This escalates into fussing and loud talk, with people almost ready to fight about it. These are issues that have happened five, ten, and even thirty years ago or longer. As long as I can remember from a child up until now, these negative specters from the past have haunted three generations, and no one can see how this has affected relationships throughout the family. For example, you can try to build a bridge to connect aunts, uncles, and cousins together, but almost at once, an aunt or uncle or cousin will blow it to pieces. This has been going on year after year.

Competition has always played a big part in my family—the West Coast versus the East Coast versus the South. Who has the biggest house or makes the most money? Who drives the biggest car or truck? Who gives the biggest gift? I must tell you that the first cousins never thought they were in competition. They were happy for one another's many achievements, and they would celebrate each other.

The aunts would regularly persuade some of the cousins to think that the other cousins were competing. They would say things like "She thinks that she is better" or "He thinks he is better because he has this or she has that." There has never been a time that we as a family have come together and laughed and had a good time. It seems if everyone feels positive about things, the good old days of fond memory and laughing and enjoying each other, soon someone brings up the negative past, wearing the scars of pain and hurt of what someone had done to Grandma Mae Mae, Grandpa Paul, uncles or aunts, and cousins…nothing happening today but instead the haunted past of yesterday.

Now year after year we say that we are going to come and bring the family together and forget about the past. We do come together, but the past still shows up. It is okay to remember the things of the past if they put a smile on your face and give you that good feeling of happiness.

I believe that we have relived the past so much that it is always a part of our future. The scar tissue is so deeply embedded in our hearts and minds that that we have become numb to the fact that it was yesterday, holding onto things that we cannot change, trying to figure out *what happened* and *why* to things that don't matter—issues and problems that are so far gone—involving loved ones who have passed on and yet people are still not getting over it. Over and over, we find ourselves stuck in time, which has caused our family to be divided against themselves. There is always a war going on, and we are so busy thinking about yesterday that we allow today to slip by without focus for tomorrow. We are stuck in a time that we can't change, looking backward instead of reaching forward and embracing change, not realizing that change can be good. We are stuck behind a wall within themselves when the door to freedom stands wide open.

My Hurt Unveiled

As you grow from a little girl to a teenager to a young lady to a beautiful young woman, you are filled with so many wonderful expectations of how you want your life to be or not to be. You pretty much have an idea of how you want to map out your life. Never imagining failures, I wanted more than anything to be successful in life.

There was always a battle in my mind, wanting things to get better between my mother and father. I loved them both, and I was always trying to figure things out. I saw that when we had death in our family, everybody would be instantly loving and concerned about one another, always trying to lend a helping hand for that moment. As a little girl, I used to pray and ask God to take my life so that my mother and father would become closer and loving toward each other and so that my brothers wouldn't have to deal with the fighting, the yelling, and the police coming to the house for their protection…that they might feel safe. No one knows how it feels to cry when nobody sees your tears or your pain or your fears of not knowing what else to do.

I tried so hard to go to school and concentrate, learning all that I could. That wasn't easy. My mind would always hold thoughts of words that my father had told me during my elementary years—"I am going to kill your mother tonight"—as I saw him lay the gun on the table. Every day I would go to school afraid of coming home to see the yellow tape around the house and police cars blocking the street. I tried hard not to think about it, but when the last bell would ring and school was out, my heart would be racing. I would get my younger brother, who went to the same school. The school was just a couple of blocks away, but when that bell rang and we were walking home, it felt like miles away. I tried hard not to let my friends or the teachers know what I was dealing with. If anyone asked me, I would act like my life was wonderful on the outside—while on the inside I wanted to die. As a little girl, this was a great burden for me to deal with.

Here I was, a teenager, yet still carrying painful memories of elementary school in middle school years, the drama still going on between my parents. The beatings stopped, but the yelling and the threats did not. I just learned to deal with it.

Going to church helped; the singing took me to another place of happiness. The more I got involved, though, the more I felt rejected by people who simply didn't know what I was dealing with, and I didn't think they cared enough to ask. This was just another issue that I had to deal with: The more I tried to be accepted by these church people, the more they seemed to push me away. I just couldn't understand why I was here.

I graduated from high school, but it was a struggle. I wonder, *Did anyone see my tears?* A young man who lived across the street from me was my high school boyfriend. He saw all my hurts, pain, and tears, and I hated when we broke up. I felt that he should have been more understanding. He knew what I had gone through and should have realized that being intimate— taking our relationship to the next level—was not to my interest at that time. I had to remember that this was high school.

I moved out of state from the West Coast to the East Coast, and what a cultural shock. People back East talked, walked, and did everything fast— straight and to the point, no beating around the bush, everyone in a rush moving and doing something. What I most liked about the East Coast was the realness. If people liked you, they liked you. If not, they would let you know right up front: *I don't like you*, and you didn't even have to second-guess. Wow.

I liked people who were real because I knew where I stood with them.

While I was back East, I was staying with my aunt whom I took as my second mother, Aunt Misty. I was able to find a good job in the banking industry and was able to go to a business college, just trying to make life a little better for myself. It wasn't long before the drama started here. I saw an AD in the newspaper for an airlines reservations clerk—*will train, previous customer service experience required*—so I applied for the job. I had always wanted to work for the airline industry. I had heard that employees got discounted airfare, and there were a lot of places I wanted to travel to.

I must have worked four to five days before I ran into my aunt Misty, the one I was living with; she also worked there. I wanted her to be surprised and happy for me. She was surprised, all right, and upset about me working at the same company. When I got home, she told me that I was messing with her bread and butter and that she was going to tell HR that I was her niece and that she didn't want me to work there. I smiled, but the next day, I went to work, clocked in, sat down at my cubicle, and had just got my headset on when I got tapped on the shoulder by my supervisor, who told me that HR wanted to see me. I said okay. I went upstairs and saw my aunt talking with one of the HR reps. As she walked out, she said, "I know you're going to do the right thing regarding this mess."

I walked in, and they asked me if I knew Misty, and I said yes. They asked how we were related. I didn't want to answer because I knew that relatives were not supposed to work together. However, because we worked in different departments, had different last names, and didn't look alike, I did not think that it would really matter. This was what I really wanted to do—work for the airlines. I told the truth because my aunt Misty had already told them that she was my mom's sister, and she told them that I used my other aunt's address and that I lived with her. So they terminated me that day.

I was so hurt. It was snowing and very cold. While I waited for the bus, tears started to run down my face. Nobody knew how I was feeling. No one saw my tears.

When I got to my stop, it was very foggy. I looked around; nobody was outside or driving by. I kept walking, and when I got close to Aunt Misty's house, I saw all my clothes outside getting snowed on. I tried to use my key to get in, but the locks had been changed, and Aunt Misty wasn't at home. So I went to her friend's house—I was friends with her friend's kids—and knocked on the door. Their mother, Kaye, told me to get away from her house. I said, "I just need to use your phone."

Kaye said, "No, you are bad news," and she closed the door in my face.

Her son yelled out the window and said, "I am sorry, Ms. GiGi. I wish I could let you in."

By now my hands were frozen. I saw another one of the neighbors. Ms. Sara had just got home, and she said, "GiGi, what are you doing outside in all this cold weather?"

I said, "I just need to use your phone."

She replied, "Did you leave your key in the house?" I said yes because I did not want her to know that my aunt Misty had put me out. All I wanted was to call my aunt Punkin at work. I told her what had happened. She came and picked me up and helped me shake all the snow off my clothes and shoes and drove me to her home, where she lived with two other aunts. My aunt Peaches told me that I couldn't stay there, and the two aunts began to fuss and argue. That made me very uncomfortable and sad inside, but again, no one could see my tears.

So I called my mother and father. My father told me to call his brother, Uncle Peanut, to come and get me. I was happy when Uncle Peanut came to pick me up and was also sad to know that my aunts were feuding over me and a job, which I had lost, though I was still in school. Yes, I did find another job.

Then, while I was living with Uncle Peanut and his family, about three months later, my uncle moved out of his home and left me there with his wife and children. It was okay at first, but then the drama started again. There was always something going on.

I would hear his wife talking about me to her sister, and that made me feel very uncomfortable. I never knew why he left, and it wasn't my business, so I tried to stay out of the way.

That was where I met my first husband, Eddie. He was my cousin's friend, and he lived down the street. He saw how my family was treating me and offered to help me so I could finish school, but that just didn't happen. So I left and came back home to the wild, wild West. After Eddie and I had built a long-distance relationship, we crisscrossed the country to visit each other. A year later, I married Eddie.

I really didn't know what I was getting myself into. Everything I was running away from, I ran right into. *Why is this happening to me?* I asked God. *What am I doing wrong?* This question I asked myself over and over. Eddie started off being very nice until we got married. All the abuse, lies, fussing, and the fighting was overwhelming for me. I guess you can say I really didn't know him and he didn't see my tears; he only caused more pain. I should have collected more data from him, understanding who he really was or what he wanted in life, He was just a man who I married whom I lost my virginity to. This was new to me. No one shared with me what love was about, not even intimacy or what to expect.

Four years later, I got married again, this time to a man named Owen. I will never forget this moment. At this time, I must have been married to Owen about four years when my grandfather Paul passed away, and I was dealing with a lot of drama from my family. A lot of things that were said and done didn't make any sense to me. I was upset because my grandfather had passed away, and some members of my family said some very hurtful things to me.

When it was time for us to leave, my cousin Mike, who was like a brother to me, flew back with me from the funeral. When we arrived at the airport, his wife picked him up, and my husband, Owen, was late picking me up. When he finally picked me up and we got home, I went to put my bags in my closet and put on my house shoes. I noticed that all of Owen's clothes were gone. I looked in the dresser drawers, and they were empty. When I turned around, he was gone. I called him on his cell phone and asked him what was going on. He said, "Sorry, I just had to leave."

I asked, "Why? I just got back from burying my grandfather, and my mother and my kids are still there. Why are you doing this?"

He said, "Look, I got to go," and he hung up the phone. I didn't understand. I didn't have an argument with him. I had been gone only a week, and it wasn't a vacation. I just couldn't understand what was going on.

I began to cry. And the devil began to talk to me. It felt like everything and everyone was coming against me, and the pressure was so heavy, I couldn't take it anymore. I wanted to kill myself and end it all. I didn't have any pills to take. I was just hurting… my heart was hurting, and no one saw my tears.

I called one of my closest friends, who was a deacon's wife in the church. I poured out my heart, crying and asking her to help me, telling her what the devil was telling me to do to myself. She said, "Look, I got company. Let me call you back later."

At that moment, I had a sharp knife in my hand, and I was going to cut the veins by my wrist and let it bleed. By the time my family came home from Alabama, I would be gone. I fell on the kitchen floor and cried until I couldn't cry anymore. Then I heard the voice of God speaking to me, and I began to feel a peace. It felt like a blanket had covered my whole body as I lay on the kitchen floor. I began to feel God's love for me, and the more I felt God's love for me, the more I felt empowered with his strength and the more I felt I could make it. *Why take your life when I gave my life for you so that you can live?* I got up off the floor, and God wiped my tears. I took my clothes off and went to bed.

Two days later my husband, Owen, came back and moved his stuff back in. Neither my mother nor my kids ever knew he had moved out and come back. However, the pain of the wound was there, with a scab on it. Deep in my mind, I really couldn't trust him anymore. I kept this a secret because of the thought of what people would say or think about me. This had been always buzzing around in my head: what they didn't know about me, they couldn't use to hurt me. The deacon's wife never did call back.

One of Ten
(Psychology and Sociology)

My mother Summer was born September 30, 1943. The sickest of the ten, she had a lot of attention due to her illness. She could not keep food down until she was about thirteen. The doctor said that she was a miracle child.

She was very smart in school, the top of her class. She knew what she wanted to be in life: a telephone operator so that she could talk all over the world to different people. Now as a child in those days, she did not have a phone in the home. My mother's desire to be a telephone operator sounded a little far-fetched to the other siblings, but she had her life all planned out. She wanted to get married and have four children, two boys and two girls, and be a telephone operator.

As years went by, my mother graduated from high school and moved to New York with her older siblings. There she met a young man and became pregnant. Soon she was an unwed mother. She wanted to be married, but her baby's father felt that he was too young to get married. Being a young mother living in the big city, trying to make a life for herself and her son, she found that this was a very hard task. So she gave her firstborn son to her older sister to raise until she could find a better life. She lived with her step-grandmother, and from time to time, things just weren't the way she wanted them to be.

She decided to make the biggest move of her life. She had stayed in touch with her high school sweetheart, and she moved to California to be with him. She found a job and got her own place, and in the meantime, she became pregnant for the second time. She and my father got married, and soon after, I was born. Things started to get a little rough. My father had a son who was nine months older than I was. Then he got the same woman pregnant again, just being a cheater. So he decided that we needed to move back East, get my mother's firstborn son, my brother, and have a new beginning as a family.

My father started to drink and became very abusive by slapping and beating my mother. He would tell her he was sorry, and they would make up. She never told her parents or older siblings what was going on. One of her youngest sisters asked if she could come and be a babysitter while my parents were at work. My mother thought that things would get better with her sister in the home; she didn't think that my father would hit her again.

Then she became pregnant again, and while she was carrying the baby, my father would beat her until she thought she had lost the baby. My father was a very jealous man. He would talk to other women and mess around with them, even sleep with them, but if he thought that someone looked at my mother and she smiled, he would think that she was messing around, and he would go and get drunk, come home, and beat her.

One time he had beat her until she was not able to stand the sunlight from the window. He messed her face up so much that we were afraid of her. Because my mother was a very light-skinned woman, her scars looked worse.

We were four and seven years old and really didn't know what was going on. We simply loved Mommy and Daddy anyway. But my father was always sending mixed messages. He always said he was sorry, and they would act like nothing ever happened. After a few years of this abuse, my mother decided that she needed time to get her head together and decide what she was going to do—stay with my father or leave. In the meantime, my mother gave us to our grandmother to raise. Then my mother and father split up, and he moved back to California.

Now my mother had three of her sisters living with her. They all worked and tried to make a good life for themselves. My mother did become a telephone operator. But as the years went by, the sisters just could not get along. They began to nag and talk about each other like they were not related. Things again became very stressful and intense. My mother didn't know if she could trust her sisters; in some ways, she was dealing with almost the same situation as with my father—verbally and mentally, if not physically.

My mother and father got back in touch, and he said that he wanted to become a family again. So my mother picked up my younger brother from my grandmother, and a year later, she picked me up. She decided if she was going to be disrespected by her own family and lied about, she might as well go back to her husband. The mental abuse from the family and physical abuse from her husband both felt the same. Yet she was seeking for real love—a love that was not given to her as a child. The only time she felt really loved was when she was sick.

The abuse continued until I was thirteen. I finally told my father that I would kill him if he hit my mother again. I said it with unrestrained anger, and at that time, I meant it—enough was enough. My father seemed disappointed as he looked into the anger-filled eyes of Daddy's little girl. For a while after this, when my father would go to sleep, I would just stand over him and give him this look. He would wake up, and I would just stare at him. Eventually he did not want to go to sleep while I was around.

The beatings stopped, and he never hit my mother again. However, the cheating, which was a part of the generational cycle, continued until the day he died. My mother loved him forever and always believed that God was going to change him. Life did get better for the both of them before he passed. And I will say my mother experienced a real love from him before he died.

Gisele's Question—Why?

I watched the families on many television shows as a child—*The Cosby Show*, *The Brady Bunch*, *The Jeffersons*, *Good Times*, *Leave It to Beaver*. As I watched all these shows on TV, I wanted my parents to be loving and happy with each other, just like on the shows.

Only God knows all the hell and drama that we had to go through. I was always asking myself so many questions: Why couldn't we be a happy family? Why can't we be a happy family? Why did my father say that he was going to kill my mother? Why did my father cheat on my mother? Why don't my mother and father like spending time with us? Why is it all about work? Why is it hard for my parents to say that they love us? Why is home so painful? Why does my mother work all the holidays—Thanksgiving, Fourth of July, Easter, our birthdays, Christmas? Why as a child, did I never know what it felt like to blow out candles on a birthday cake or to have a birthday party like all the other kids I knew?

When my parents broke up, my mother would send my brothers and me to live with her mother and father, my grandparents. As a child, I heard my grandmother talking about my mother and father, and it seemed like we were just a burden to her. I often spoke up and asked my grandmother, "Why do you always talk about my mother and father?" And just as often, I got beat for talking and asking my grandmother too many questions.

She would always say, "A child needs to stay in a child's place." It was always hard to do that if anyone talked about my parents in a negative way. And every time my grandmother beat me, she would say, "Mama is beating you because she loves you." So whether I did something bad or just spoke up to my grandmother, she would beat me and always tell me that same old story: "I'm just beating you because I love you." So I asked her to hate me, because if she hated me, then she wouldn't beat me so much.

As I got older, I saw that my father beat my mother, but the next day, they would be lovey-dovey, and I just could not understand. He beat my mother, and then they loved each other more, so did beating mean love? My grandmother said she beat me because she loved me, so I felt that my father must really love my mother because he would really beat her, and the next day it would be like nothing had really happened. My mother really loved him.

As I was growing up, this was always going through my subconscious mind. Beating is showing you a form of love. But beating doesn't feel good. Why doesn't love feel good?

I became an adult and married at a very early age, nineteen. My parents gave me a big wedding. I loved my husband, but I was in love with somebody else, an old boyfriend who lived across the street. He was always there for me. When my parents fought or the police came to our house, which was very often, he would always hug me and kiss me, tell me that everything was going to be okay, and at last make me smile.

When I was in high school, surrounded by hormones at an all-time high, I was afraid to have sex. My boyfriend, whom I was in love with, wanted sex, but I just wasn't ready for that. The peer pressure came from his friends telling him, "If GiGi is not giving you sex, then you don't need to be with her." So we broke up, and he dated other girls and had sex with them. I was still in love with him. I did date other guys, but he was always my number 1 guy. It did hurt me when we broke up.

As years went by, I moved back East and met a young man, Eddie, and we decided we were going to get married. I moved back to California and was in the mall doing some last-minute shopping, about to be married, when I ran into my old boyfriend whom I was still in love with. He asked me what I had been up to, and I told him I was getting married. He said, "I know we are getting married."

"No, I am marrying a man from the East Coast."

He said, "No, you are marrying me." So I told him if he didn't believe me, he could ask my mother; all the invitations had gone out. Before I could get home, he was parked at my house talking with my mother, asking her if it was true that I was getting married. My mother told him yes, it was true. So he asked me to marry him. My heart was saying yes, but my mind was saying, *No, you have sent invitations out, and your fiancé and his friends are already here.* He asked me again not to marry this man, because he loved me, and he wanted to marry me. He asked me to hug and kiss him. I said no even though my heart said yes. So I walked away because my mind didn't want to forget that he had gotten a girl pregnant and that he had had sex with different partners while I was a virgin.

No one really told me what love was all about, and I wanted to get away. My parents would fuss and fight, break up, and make up like nothing had ever happened. So I picked my wedding day to be in the month of August because my grandparents got married August 17, and they had been married more than fifty years. So I thought that I was going to have this longevity of a happy marriage.

Being young, I was clearly confused. I thought that choosing the same wedding month as my grandparents would make a difference in my life. I thought that I was going to have this long and happy marriage.

Now on my wedding day, my oldest brother told me that I didn't have to do this. I don't know if he saw my mind or my heart speaking out. As my father walked me down the aisle, he told me that I did not have to do this. Even when the minister asked, "Who gives this woman to be married?" my father stood there, whispering in my ear, "You don't have to do this. We could just have a party. Don't worry about the money being spent." I stood there as confused as I could be. *I love this man, but I am in love with another.* Growing up in a confused environment makes your head cloudy, and when your head is cloudy, you can't think clearly, and you make wrong decisions, thinking you are doing the right thing.

After I got married, a couple of months went by while I was trying to get settled in. Eddie's house phone kept ringing. He told me not to answer it because bill collectors were calling. One day I called my aunt, and she said that she would call me right back. When the phone rang, I answered it, and a lady was on the other end asking me who I was. I told her who I was, and she began to cry. I asked her what was wrong. She gave me a long story about how she and my husband were supposed to be married, but he had left her at the altar.

I really didn't know what to say because it was becoming clear that everything he told me about his house, the car, and so on was a lie. So when he came home, I asked him about this lady and questioned him about some of the things she had told me were hers—like the car. He said it was his, and when I asked him to tell me the truth, he slapped me across the face. Then he grabbed me and said that he was going to really hurt me if I mentioned that woman to him again.

At this time, I was silently crying out: *Help! I married my father. What am I going to do?* He came to me and said he was sorry and that this would never happen again. Months went by, and I kept catching this man in lies. Every time I did, though, he would hit me, and we would fight. I wanted to leave, but I stayed because I was afraid to leave, afraid of being a failure. My parents had paid out so much for my wedding, and some people had said that my marriage wasn't going to last. I found myself trying to prove them wrong and wanting to believe that things were going to get better.

My youngest brother, Billy, came to live with me. I was happy, and I felt safe because he was tall and very strong and not afraid of anyone. While Billy was out, Eddie and I had a fight, and he bruised my face. I locked myself in the bathroom until he left.

When Billy got home, I came out of the bathroom. When Billy saw my face, he wanted to fight Eddie. I told him no because I didn't want him to go to jail behind this person who wasn't worth it. I felt that my brother would have killed him. When Eddie came home, he saw the anger in Billy's eyes. He didn't say anything; they just stared each other down. However, Eddie knew that the look my brother gave meant that if this happened again, Eddie had better run for his life.

I never wanted to tell my father because I knew that if I did, my husband would be a dead man. My father did not want anyone to beat or hit me or say the wrong thing to me. I was Daddy's little girl. My father would call me back East and check whether everything was all right. I would always say, "Yes, Daddy, everything is fine." My father would always ask if Eddie had ever hit me, and I would always say, "No, Daddy, you know if anyone ever hit me, I would let you know." My father said that if Eddie ever did hit me, I should just tell him, and he would take care of him.

Things still did not get better. I started working at a bank as a teller. For this job, I always wanted to look my best—hair, makeup, and all the rest. I also worked a part-time job in a grocery store, balancing cashier drawers. One day, I had just gotten paid, and I had direct deposit. I called off sick on my part-time job and went to the ATM to withdraw some cash—but it said I had insufficient funds. So I tried again, with the same result.

I went to my supervisor about my check not being deposited, but when he printed out my account, it showed that I'd had a direct deposit, and I had had two large ATM withdrawals. I said, "No, that can't be true, because I was unable to get money out." I checked to see what ATM was used for this transaction, and the camera showed that Eddie's friend had taken a large sum of money out and so had Eddie.

When I came home, Eddie and his friends were freebasing in my apartment. And I asked them to leave and get out of my house. Nobody moved. I told them I was going to call the police if they did not leave. Everyone jumped up and started to leave.

I asked Eddie why he took all my money out of my account and why he gave his friend my card and code to the ATM. He got really upset and said if I did not leave he was going to kill me. I asked him why again. He went into the bedroom and got a gun, and I began to run as fast as I could while he was loading the gun. He was unable to catch me.

I got into my car and drove to my brother-in-law's and sister-in-law's house and asked them to help me. I told them what had happened, and Eddie's brother then went over to my apartment to talk to him. The next day, I came home. He said he was sorry and this would never happen again. He never pulled a gun on me again; however, the fighting didn't stop. I decided to move back to California where I felt safe and where I knew that Eddie was not going to hit me because he was afraid of what my father might do to him if he ever found out. I never did tell my father about the beatings.

On January 13, 1990, my father passed away. I was very sad. I was pregnant with my son, just trying to deal with the shocking death of my father and knowing that he would never see my child or children. My father was gone, and I was pregnant and living with an abusive husband who wanted to pick up beating me where he had left off. He would get mad at me for silly things. If I asked him to pick up something to eat after work, he would get mad at me and cuss me out. And when he came home, he would be ready to fight, yelling and pushing me against the wall.

Some nights, while I was in bed, he would just pull my hair. It almost felt like he was going to break my neck, he was pulling so hard. My unborn son would kick and move almost as if he was trying to protect me. And I would just cry and pat my stomach and tell my baby it was going be okay.

One night when I was about eight months pregnant, it was late, and I kept tossing and turning. My husband said, "Look, I'm trying to get some sleep. Stop all this moving." I jumped up and ran to the bathroom. I began to throw up, and it seemed like I wasn't going to stop. I was weak and very sick.

My brother Chuck, visiting from northern California, heard the uproar and came to help me while my husband lay in the bed and did nothing. At this time, Chuck began to see my husband for who he really was. Eddie would always put on a front when my brothers and father were around. Chuck felt sorry for me.

Now it was time for me to have the baby. We got to the hospital, and I was scared because this was all new. I was finally going to see the little person inside me. My aunt also was there with me. My husband wanted to leave me at the hospital because, he said, he was tired. I begged him to stay. He said, "I'll be right back," and walked out of the room. At that moment, my water broke, and he walked back five minutes later.

I had my son. I didn't even get to stay overnight in the hospital. I was admitted at five o'clock in the morning and discharged by that evening. I asked my doctor if I was going to stay overnight. He said that there were no complications and no beds available. It was a full day.

This was my first child, and I didn't know anything. Two days later, I was sitting on the sofa feeding my son when my husband came home and asked me what was for dinner. I said, "Dinner," not having given it a thought.

Mind you, I was still sore from having the baby, so I said, "Can you just eat some leftovers that my aunt cooked?" He walked over and slapped me so hard that my son fell out of my arms and hit the floor. Thank God the floor was carpeted. And he started yelling at me, and my son was crying.

My aunt came in the room and started yelling, "I'm going to call the police if you don't leave." He left and came back later that night. I slept downstairs while he slept upstairs. You would think that he would want to sleep nearby so that he could help with the baby. No, my little cousin Mike, whom my mother had raised as my brother, slept on the floor next to me and helped me.

A year later, I found out that Eddie was cheating on me. He called me from his job, working for a big hospital, and said that he had to work overtime and that he was tired and hungry. He asked me to cook some pork chops, and I did just that. I finished cooking dinner and called his job to let him know that I was bringing it over. The people I talked to told me that he wasn't there. He was gone for the day.

I thought maybe it was an oversight because he had called and said that a lot of accident victims had come in, and they needed him to stay to help. I drove to the hospital where Eddie worked, and his car was parked there, so I just knew it was an oversight. I got to the OR department and spoke with a supervisor, who told me that there were no trauma victims. It was a slow night, and my husband had left early. He checked the time card to verify that this was correct. So I went back home and waited for him.

When he arrived home, he said that he was tired and told me how busy the hospital was. He took a shower and then asked what I had cooked. I told him, "The pork chops, like you asked." He saw that

I had packed a lunch bag for him. He asked why the food was in the bag, and I said that I had made it for him to eat at work, but he had not been there.

I started upstairs, but before I was all the way in the bedroom, he grabbed my hair and slammed me down on the bed. He held a rusty pair of scissors up to my throat. I could feel the pinching of it on my neck. He asked why I was checking up on him. "I was just being a good wife."

He said, "Say something else. I'm going to kill you. Your daddy isn't here to save you, and now what are you going to do?"

All I could do was say, "Jesus, Jesus, Jesus." I know that there is power in the name of Jesus. He jumped off me and got in his car and left. He was gone about a week, and when he came back, the locks on the doors were changed. I filed for my divorce, and I never looked back—this chapter of my life was over.

I Hate You!

Hate is a feeling of strong dislike or anger. I felt it after seeing my father cheat on my mother and then come home and lie about his whereabouts. We had seen him give money to his nieces and nephews, just blowing money, being "big time," every body's favorite uncle. In the meanwhile, his children wanted or needed money, love, and support in their lives, but that was something he couldn't give to his very own. All that he could give was a lot of painful memories that will always play back in our minds.

Then when I was in the eleventh grade, I was walking home with my friends, and it was very hot. My mother was at work, and my friends and I were wishing we could get a ride from school. My father passed us walking with another woman with her kids. I waved at him, but he just sped up. I knew that he had seen us, but he was hoping that we hadn't seen him.

Later that night, my father just looked at me as if he wanted to say something, and I said nothing to him. What kind of father would do this to his only daughter? I became very angry and bitter at my father to the point that I didn't want to be in his presence. He would walk in the front door, and I would walk out the back door. He could sit down in a chair and get up, but I didn't even want to sit in the same seat he sat in.

I always wondered if my mother was tired of the games that my dad played. Even if she wasn't, I was! I was embarrassed at going over to my aunt's house and seeing him hugged up with another woman, hearing my cousins talk about what my father had done, or having people at school telling me things about my father. I was angry and upset and just wanted to get away.

Trying to understand people was a lot of work for me. People will say one thing and do another. They will smile in your face and stab you in the back. They will lie to you, even though they know the truth. People say, "Sticks and stones will break your bones but words will never hurt you." But not only will words hurt you; words can destroy you. As a youth dealing with so many issues with people, sometimes I wondered if anyone was sane, or was everyone crazy?

When I went to schools that my older brother Chuck attended also, teachers would expect me to be like him. He was very smart and knew everything, always had an answer. There was nothing wrong with that, but I was a different person. I'm not saying that I wasn't smart, but I didn't feel as smart as my big brother. Even when we would go to church, people would always compare me to him. Sad to say, my family did the same thing.

I never understood why people would do this. However, I would just move on and act like it didn't bother me. I would say to myself, "They just don't know me!" This was just another layer of bricks added to the wall I was building around my heart, so the pain could just disappear behind the wall. I tried so hard to hide the anger, disappointment, and bitterness and not to overlook the tears. I would ask, "Why am I here? Why does love hurt so bad? Will people ever see the real me? Does anyone care to know me? Am I just here to be used by other people?"

When you have all of these feelings going on inside, you become a little bit dysfunctional. You're trying to make sense out of all the things you are dealing with, and yet still nothing makes sense. I remember many baffling incidents that occurred in my life. One Thanksgiving my mother started her dinner early, went to work for an eight-hour shift, and then came home and finished the rest. My father had gone out all day, visiting family and drinking; that was the norm for him every holiday. I always hated that. It was okay to visit, but the drinking…

and I say he was drinking because when he came home, he was drunk! My mother asked us, "Did your dad come home since he left early this morning?"

I said, "No."

"I have been calling him all day asking him what time he was coming home, and he would always say, 'I will be there in five minutes.'" Since we lived so close to our relatives, it should've only taken him five minutes, but it took him five hours. When he walked into the house, you could smell the alcohol on his breath.

I asked my father, "What took you so long?" My brothers and I were dressed, and we had been waiting for him to come and get us as he had told us he would. We had waited so long because we wanted to visit with the family too and come back in time before our mother returned from work so that we could eat Thanksgiving dinner together. My dad just walked away.

My mother said, "You know these kids were waiting for you." As my father grabbed a beer from the refrigerator, she asked, "Why are you drinking another beer? You look like you have had too many already!" My father started cursing at my mother, calling her out of her name.

My mother screamed, "How could you stand up here and look into my face and say these things to me? You know what I had to do! I worked, came home, and finished a nice dinner for us, and you are too drunk to enjoy it!"

My father replied, "I don't care about this stuff!" and started throwing the food my mother had cooked outside on the ground. He said, "If you say another word, I'm going to kill all of you!" My mother did have to get the last word in, and my father ran into the bedroom and got his gun. My mother, my brother, and I ran out of the house.

As we were running, I saw the sweet potato pies stepped on, and I stood there in disbelief. My mother was yelling, "Come on, come on!" It was raining outside, and we ran since my mother didn't have her license yet.

We ran until we saw a phone booth. My mother gave me a dime to call my father's baby sister, who only lived a few blocks away, to see if she and my uncle would come and talk to my father. She said, "No, I don't have time for all of that." I begged her, but she said no and hung the phone up.

My mother was in another phone booth talking to my father's best friends, Uncle Roseborough and Aunt Jewel; they were having a big dinner at their house. My mother told them that she didn't want to bother them; however, my father was acting crazy, and we were stranded at a phone booth in fear of my father and what he had said about killing us. So Uncle Roseborough told us, "Stay right there. We are on our way."

It seemed like it took them a long time to get where we were. We lived on the east side, and they lived on the west side. They were only twenty minutes away, but those twenty minutes felt like hours. Just imagine it's Thanksgiving, and everyone else is at home eating and enjoying the holiday, yet you are standing in a phone booth in the rain.

When I saw my uncle and aunt, I was extremely happy to see them. They drove us to our house, where my father was sitting in the living room watching TV with the gun on the sofa, as though nothing was wrong. My uncle and my father walked into another room and talked. Then both my parents went out of the room and talked awhile. My older brother and I tried to clean up the mess that my father had made with our Thanksgiving dinner, scattered over the floor and the ground outside. Wow, what a Thanksgiving dinner!

By this time, we wished our father had stayed where he was. I hated him for that: every holiday he would get drunk and start a fight with my mother. I just couldn't understand this type of behavior. My parents fought all the time, but on holidays, you would hope things would be different. As a child you wonder, *Am I asking for too much?*

I recall another time when my brothers and I were at home on a Saturday evening. We were waiting for my mother to come home and take us shopping. Then after we had gone shopping and the food was put away, my mother began cooking. My father came home angry, and he slammed the front door.

We were watching TV, and he told us to turn it off. We didn't understand why, and Mother said, "Turn that TV back on." By this time, we were scared, so my mother stopped what she was doing, came into the living room, and turned the TV back on.

My father then turned the stereo on as loud as it would go. We couldn't even hear the TV. So I asked my father, "Why are you playing the stereo so loud?"

He told me, "Shut up and grab me a beer." I gave him the beer, and he drank it, not saying anything. Then he threw the can on the floor. My mother came into the living room and turned the stereo down. My younger brother was walking by the table where my father was. (Remember, he kept a gun on the table next to him.) My father told my brother to pick up the can that he had thrown on the floor. When my younger brother was about to pick it up, my father said, "If you pick up that can, I'm going to blow your brains out." My brother stood there confused, not knowing what to do.

We all were scared except for my mom—and myself, it seems. I asked my dad, "Why would you want to blow his brains out if he picked up the can that you threw on the floor?"

He replied, "You better go and sit your black butt down somewhere, and I am tired of you asking me questions." My brother and I just stood there looking at him, my brother being only eight or nine years old at the time.

My mother said to my father, "If you're going to blow his brains out, just do it!" She turned off the stove, grabbed her purse, and said she was going to call the police.

But my father had the phones. He got up, went into the kitchen, and told my brother, "Come on, let's go." My father had just turned around when I started to run, but right before I could get out the door, something flew by my head and knocked a hole in the wall. My father had thrown his shoe.

We went to the neighbor's house across the street and called the police. By the time the police arrived, my father was gone. They looked at the wall and said to my mother, "Your daughter is really lucky. If this shoe could knock a hole into this drywall and if had hit your daughter's head, it would have done some damage to her, and we would've looked at this as a different type of report."

This constant mental abuse went on for years. We were dealing with a father who had married a good woman and acted as though he hated having kids. He portrayed this perfect family to the outsider, the perfect son, the outstanding brother, the world's greatest uncle, and the best dad ever to everyone else that knew him, but behind closed doors, if only the walls could speak, the story they would tell. Many nights were fearful, when we were afraid to fall asleep, not knowing what might happen in the middle of the night.

Many times from elementary school, junior high school, through ninth grade, I tried to find some understanding of why my father did what he did, trying to find where this anger came from. He had a good wife, good kids, good income; many days and nights I asked myself, *Why must we live in torment?* Why did it feel like every other weekend we had to go to hell, and those weekends that we didn't, we had already gone there the week before? The older I grew, the stronger the root of hate that was embedded and growing inside of me. I would hate at times to see my dad come home. I hated to hear his voice, I hated his scent, and I hated my own features that reminded me of him.

I hated to be around family members who spoke highly of him due to the fact that it was hard to see the good in him. He never demonstrated that good toward us. Many times I just looked at him, and we would have a staring match. He didn't know what I was thinking, and I didn't know what he was thinking. I had become very hard and numb, bitter and empty. I would often see other little girls with their fathers, and I could only dream and hope that my father would treat me the way other fathers treated their Daddy's little girls.

At this stage of my life, there weren't too many things I was happy about. I was mad at my father for doing the things that he had done to us and mad at my mother for putting up with his foolishness. I was mad at the teachers at school and at church for not understanding me. I was reaching for something to hold on to. When I reached out for love, hate and bitterness were always there. I reached out for understanding and found only confusion and disappointment. I reached out for peace, but war and trouble were always there. Somewhere deep inside me was a little piece of faith, hoping and believing that a better day was coming.

It Won't Happen to Me

Wham, bam—thank you, ma'am. As a young adult, having two children and being a single mom was not the plan that I wanted for my life. My children, yes; being single, no. I always wanted to be married and in a loving relationship. I had a dream that I was always holding on to, never wanting to be alone. I felt that after all the things I had gone through as a child and in my first marriage, I deserved someone to really love me the way I needed to be loved. I wondered, *Am I asking for too much?*

When I got pregnant with my daughter, I wasn't married. I had slipped and slept with a "friend." He talked a lot about his family and how he felt that he was the black sheep. His brothers had kids, and he never was never able to produce a child. He took me out to nice restaurants, wined and dined me, and took me to plays. He was just a good friend. However, that good friend turned on me. He had asked me to go to a New Year's Eve party with him at his brother's house. I told him that I wanted to go to church for Watch Night Service. He said, "I will go with you."

I said, "Fine, after church I will go with you to your brother's."

He said, "I won't stay long. I just want to show my face." Once we got to his brother's house, it was very warm. I asked him for some punch. Whatever was in that punch, it got me very sleepy. I told him I was ready to go home, so we left.

As we were riding in his car, he said, "It's getting very late. Instead of taking you to your house, why don't you stay at my house? I have four bedrooms. You can stay in one of them."

I said, "No, I think I better go home." I was feeling lightheaded.

He said, "I will just take you home in the morning." And I said okay. At that time, all I wanted was to go to bed. We arrived at his house, and he showed me the room and told me if I needed anything to let him know. Then he closed the door behind him. I took my dress off and got in the bed.

The next thing I knew, he had come back into the room and was kissing and touching me. I told him, "Stop, I'm not on any birth control." But one thing led to another. When I insisted that I wanted to go home, he agreed. So I went home. I was very disappointed in myself and fearful of what had just happened.

But that good friend turned on me. Weeks later when I told him that I was pregnant, he told me, "How could you be pregnant? I can't make a baby, and all the other ladies I slept with weren't able to conceive a child with me, so all I can tell you is to get an abortion, and how do I know this child is mine or not?" So he rejected me and my unborn child.

He told me, "Why won't you fall down the stairs and miscarry the baby?" He said a lot of other mean things: "I'm not going to marry you." "I have been married before." I didn't ask him to marry me.

He told me that his mother was going to be very upset, and I asked him, "Why would your mother be upset? You're a grown older man. This has nothing to do with your mother."

All I could say is, "I shouldn't be pregnant by a man who didn't want the child."

Here I was, a single woman, an entrepreneur, a hairstylist working very hard to support my child and myself with no assistance from him. I remember when my daughter was born, my mother called him from the hospital to say that I was having the baby, and he told her, "Call me when the child is born."

So my mother called him back and told him, "You need to come see your daughter, and she looks like you."

He replied, "I will come after I leave this wedding." When he got to the hospital and he saw my daughter, he said, "Wow, she has features of my mother." Mind you, I had never seen his mother. He told me that his father wanted to see my daughter, so when I came from the hospital, his father came over, and he said, "Yes, this is my granddaughter." This was the first time I had seen his father.

I will never forget my daughter's first Christmas. Her father had told me that every Christmas Eve his family had a big Christmas party. He then asked me if I wanted to go, and I said yes. He told me what time he was going to pick me up. My daughter and I were ready, but when he arrived at my house, he told me he was sorry, but his mother had told him if he brought me to the party, she was not going to participate and there wouldn't be a party. She only wanted my daughter to come.

So I took off my coat and let my daughter go. She was dressed so pretty. I couldn't believe that I would see the day when my child would be welcome to go somewhere but her mother wasn't. These people said that they were just country folks, that they loved everybody. I questioned that type of love.

Two years later, I met another young man. I thought that we had a lot in common. Everything I liked, he liked, and vice versa. I had one child with my first husband and one unwed. He also had two children, one by his ex-wife and one outside the marriage. I loved music, and he played with different artists, bands, and television shows. This gave me an opportunity to meet different celebrities. As the owner of a salon and a stylist, I was able to talk about the different celebrities and functions that I had been invited to. My life at this time was like a storybook, with never a dull moment. I felt deeply connected with him, and the passion was unbelievable.

We got married and had a large wedding. I knew something was wrong, though, when I wanted his children in the wedding, and he said that it wasn't a good idea, because their mothers both still had feelings for him. Yes, that did raise a brow. However, he told me that he was divorced, like me. His divorce had been finalized the same year as mine, just two months later, which I found amazing. I got along well with his whole family—until the baby mama drama started, which was another nightmare.

On one issue after another, my husband couldn't stand up to these woman and put his foot down to his kids! I am reminded of a Valentine's Day, which was the day before our anniversary. I had just gotten out of the hospital a few days before. We got a phone call from his daughter. She wanted him to spend Valentine's Day with her. Here I was, needing him to be with me, and this was our time of year to be together. Now, any other time would've been fine with me; he told her that, but she insisted that he came that night. She hung the phone up, and right then her sister called. When I answered the phone, the sister began to curse me out. Then the both of them were on the phone cursing and saying all sorts of things. I hung up the phone because I didn't want to hear the garbage that they were talking about.

My husband called them and told them that I was wrong and that I was trying to keep him away from them. I couldn't believe the words that were coming out of his mouth. I was so angry and upset that my stitches felt like they were ripping apart. I couldn't believe that this man couldn't stand up to his daughter and her half-sister, even though she wasn't his child. I didn't understand his kind of love for me: I was his wife, trying to recuperate from a major operation, and we were dealing with this.

From that time, every year my love for him began to fade away. Where was the man I felt so connected to, who had so much in common with me? What was happening with this picture? Where was the strong love that we shared and feelings so deep and the passion that made my heart throb? All these emotions were starting to explode within me, but all I see is cloudy days with no idea of what's to come or to expect in this fading relationship.

Could this be happening to me, another wham bam, is this a dream or a nightmare, was this not real love for me? The reality begins to set in.

Looking for Peace

As a little girl, I was brought up in church. I was told that whenever you need peace, love, happiness, or just plain help, you could find it in the church. Whether Catholic, Baptist, or Church of God in Christ (COGIC), somewhere among the different types of religion, you could always find peace and help. While I was taking this journey as a hurting little girl, my oldest brother and two of my older cousins would go out and visit different churches. Then they came back and talked about which one they liked the best. If they went more than twice to the same church, they were really into it.

Once my brother asked if I wanted to go with him to the church. He talked about how nice the people were—he felt like they were family—and how different people would play the tambourine and the piano. He was so excited about this church. It was like it took his mind off what was happening at home: the working mother, the abusing stepfather, the fighting and yelling, and all the police who came to our home every other weekend and some school nights. By contrast, this church really made him feel good inside.

There was a feeling of excitement that he had felt before at an early age while living in New York with our mother. She used to sing with a holiness church where people would sing, jump and down, clap their hands, and praise God. People used to get in a rush to get to church, and this new church had the same familiar feeling.

As we joined this little church, several members of our family began to attend. I just couldn't wait to go to church on Sunday, Wednesday, and back again on Sunday. Choir rehearsal was Saturday, Wednesday was Bible study, and Sunday was all day. Friday was young people's night.

Soon I had gotten really involved in this church. It made me push things that were hurting me far back in my mind, and I began singing in the choir. My brother used to write plays, and I would act in them. I was a part of the sunshine band and purity classes, which taught us more about Jesus at different levels. Purity class also taught us about self-esteem and early womanhood. Every organization in the church, I was involved in, and I wanted to do my very best always wanting to shine and have people accept me, love me, and say, "Good job. I am proud of you. You are going to be somebody." I guess you would say I was looking for approval. That never happened because since I was always attending faithfully, they could always count on me and even take me for granted. Remember, my brothers and I would walk to church in all types of weather. Living in California, it could get very hot, so walking to church was a big sacrifice as a child while searching for peace. I was just happy to go to church because there was no peace at home.

As I remained faithful to this church, the people started to change. No matter what I did well or how satisfying it was to me, they would change my assignment. For example, if we sang a song in the choir and I sounded good leading the song, they would say, "I think this person would do a better job." In the plays that my brother wrote, they would often take the part away from me and give it to someone who was not as good or as faithful. I was always being put on the back burner. They just didn't know that they were hurting me and adding more scars to a hurting heart.

I remember that every year with the purity class they would have a contest for king and queen. You could win a trophy, a crown, and a lot of other prizes. The winners were the ones who had raised the most money by selling candy, asking for different sponsors to donate money to help. We picked up cans in the street and turned them in to the recycling bin for cash. Even though that was the hardest job, I did it.

When I was thirteen, on the night when all monies were due to be turned in, I counted all my money. My mother counted it as well, to make sure we had the right amount, and we turned the cash in. This was so exciting to me, it was as if I was in a beauty pageant with fifty state contestants.

I had worked very hard for this moment. My mother had brought me a long beautiful dress and shoes. My hair was pressed and curled, and I was so happy. As the program continued on, finally the men who came were announcing how much money each candidate had received for all of their hard work. When they announced the money I had turned in, it was a much lower amount than we had counted. I almost passed out.

It turned out that my mother and other sponsors knew how much was given for me to win. When they announced the winner, she was shocked herself. She didn't know that she had brought in that much. One of the leaders told me that they gave part of my money to the other contestant so that she would win, and because I was younger, I could always run next year.

I was overcome by the hurt and the unreality of such doings. How could you steal from me and then smile in my face and expect me to do the hard work over again? They didn't care about a hurting little girl. They didn't love me enough to put a smile or to see the hurt on my little face.

As time went by, I was losing interest in this church. I really didn't want to be a part anymore due to they would always overlook me. Some of the members would say that I was fast because I spoke up for myself. Some said that I was going to get pregnant before I reached thirteen. I proved them wrong. I wasn't even interested in sex at that time, and I was in the dark as far as knowing what to do or how. My parents didn't tell me about sex; that subject was never mentioned in our house. I freaked out the first time my period came on; I hadn't known what to expect.

I'll never forget a certain young couple in the church. They had small kids, and the husband asked if I could watch the baby while they were doing other things in the church. I believed he was a deacon and had to count money, and his wife was an usher. I watched the baby for a couple of Sundays, and the husband gave me a few dollars.

One Sunday, it was testimony service. The wife of this deacon got up and said that there was a little sister in the church messing around with her husband and that she needed prayer. She pointed to me. Mind you, I was only thirteen years old. Everybody just looked at me. I never watched their baby again.

I could not believe that this woman got up and said such a thing to the church. *What did I do to make you think that I was messing around with your husband?* That really blew my mind. I didn't want to go to this church. I felt that these people had issues. They pretended that they had so much love for people, but they didn't have enough love to see that they were hurting a little girl and adding more scars to a wounded heart.

I moved on from this church and attended and joined other churches. As I got older, I saw that I was repeating almost the same drama of people using me in the name of the Lord. *Oh, sister, can you do this or that?* But when it came down to recognizing me for the good work, they would forget my name and not mention me on the program and always say, "I'm sorry, this will never happen again," but it did, over and over again.

My grandmother would always work very hard in church when they needed something to get done. They knew they could count on her, whether for more time or money. They knew she would be the one to count on. My grandmother was never recognized for the work she had done in the church. They always forgot her name. My mother had the same experience.

My son wanted to lead a song in the choir, and they asked who wanted to lead the song. My son kept raising his hand, and the choir director just looked past him and asked someone else to lead the song. My daughter was leading a song along with another little girl in the church. My daughter sang the song very well. Now she had been a member of this church since birth, so why did the same choir director forget to put my daughter's name on the program? And when she announced that the girls were doing the duet, she forgot my daughter's name. Now I must remind you that my children were faithful and they could always count on me to bring my kids to all church functions and being overlooked doesn't feel good. I was looking for peace in the church, but it was not what I received.

There was a time I had to be hospitalized for surgery. Right before I had my surgery, I spoke with my choir leaders and ask them to pray for me during this time. It was a major surgery, and I was a little bit fearful. Both the choir director and the minister of music said that they would be praying for me. This was the department where I volunteered faithfully for most of every Sunday. Not one of my leaders came by to visit with me, sent a card, or even called to check on me.

One couple, Sandra and Ken, came by and fixed food for my family. Trina and Mark brought flowers, and Janice, Jolene, and Carol did come by with gifts. However my leaders, in spite of my trust and faith in them, didn't show up. The excuse was that they didn't have my phone number. They expected me to believe that the sign-in sheet at every rehearsal would not tell them how to get in touch with me. However, when someone needed Sister GiGi to do something for them, they knew the right number to call.

While I was lying flat on my back, I began to talk to God my Father, and I asked him about this peace and love that people talk about in church and where I might find them. Though some may refer to a higher power, I call him Father, and he began to speak to me. He said, "Everything that you want and is looking for is in you." I stopped right there and started to take inventory. I realized that God is love and had said, "Love your neighbor as thyself." This meant that I had to start loving myself so that I could love others the way God wanted me to. In fact, if I couldn't love myself, I can't love anyone else. And if I couldn't love, others would know that I was not concerned about their well-being.

How could I say that I was a Christian? How could I go to church and not speak to my brothers and sisters? How could I sing and clap my hands or be involved in the different organizations in the church and not have love for all or just some or should I say even a few? God is *love*. And love reaches out to everyone. For God so loved the world that he gave his only Son that we may live again. So I thought about the love of God and how he loves me no matter what color or what race I belong to, how tall or small I am, any disability or dysfunctions—God still loves me. And I began to love myself and kiss and hug myself, and a big smile came on my face, I experience a peace so full that nothing else mattered. I found peace within myself, and the love overflowed through me and reached out to everyone.

The Spiritual Operation
(When the Healing Begins)

I had gone through many things in my life—a lot of them I overlooked, others I just forgot about or covered up the memories. One day when my heart was hurting and I couldn't think right, I would make wrong decisions that felt right. Everything seemed to be going out of control, so I went to the doctor, Jesus, and asked him what was wrong with me. He said, "I'm going to take you through some tests and see what the results are."

I went back into the doctor's waiting room after going through the entire faith test. I really wanted to know what was wrong with me. Dr. Jesus stepped into the room and said, *Yes, you have passed every test that was given to you. However, I did see some scar tissue that are exposed and causing pain as well as old issues that need to be removed, so I have scheduled an operation for you today.*

It was raining outside, and I said to Dr. Jesus, "The weather is bad, and there is another storm on the way." Dr. Jesus said, *I know. I already spoke to the storm and told it to be still.* I began to cry, and Dr. Jesus told me that weeping may endure for a night, *but don't worry. Joy comes in the morning.* As I felt myself getting sleepy, I heard the doctor say, *Just take my yoke upon you, and learn of me. I will give you rest.*

Dr. Jesus opened up my heart. There were so many scars that were embedded, and they had started to bleed. As he performed the surgery, he started removing the scar tissue from the past issues: disappointment, lack, discouragement, poverty, loneliness, anger, unforgiveness, and bitterness. As the doctor was removing the pain of the scar tissue, he saw a larger, deeper scar that was bleeding, causing a lot of problems. As he cut deeper to see the source of the bleeding; then, Jesus noticed that my blood was low. So he shared his blood with me.

During this operation, Dr. Jesus was able to remove Pride. At first, it was so deep that the more he cut, the deeper Pride would embed itself, causing complications for me. Jesus spoke to Pride and said, *Be still*, and pride had to obey. Jesus removed the sting and pain and left the scars to remind me that I am healed and don't have to suffer from the pain of the past. Dr. Jesus had taken out the root of the problem and healed the brokenness of my heart.

When I woke up from the operation, I felt different—I felt free. I jumped up and began to realize who I am. I am healed, I am great, I am rich, I am prosperous, I am healthy, I am happy, I am confident—I am everything I want to be and can do what I need to. I am a blessing.

I sat down, and for a moment, I started to feel a little weak, so I closed my eyes and fell asleep. When I opened my eyes, I had a visitor by the name of Fear. Fear said, *Hello?*

And I responded, "Hello."

Fear asked me how I was feeling. I took a deep breath and said, "Why are you here?"

Fear responded, *I have always been here with you. I had a home inside your heart until an earthquake came and all the walls fell down. I had to go to my vacation home because I couldn't stay any longer in that big heart of yours. All my friends were gone and would never return.*

I asked, "Where is your vacation home?"

Fear said, *Well, it's a little place in the mind. I can't stay too long, for the waves knock my little house down, and I always have to rebuild my little spot.* Fear asked me if I needed anything, so I said yes and asked Fear for everything that had been stolen from me—my dreams, my family, my home, my confidence, my career. Fear said, *When I give you all those things back, then what do you want me to do?*

I said, "Fear, you are no longer welcome in my mind, my body, or my soul."

Then Dr. Jesus spoke to Fear and said, *Fear, sorry to cut this visit short, but you have to leave now and never return.* And Fear left.

Always stay in this mind-set of who you are. Speak it out into the universe, and watch things happen for you. Be free, live life to the fullest, always expecting great things to take place in your life, and see yourself where you want to be.

Forget about yesterday. You can't change the past. However, you can start today making changes for a better tomorrow. Always remember: We win, no matter what. We are more than conquerors.

Say it, and the key is to believe it, whatever may come or go. Just believe and focus on what you want and see the results. Never doubt. Keep the *faith* alive, and Fear will never stay where Faith is.

Faith builds power within you, the expectation of things becoming real, coming into existence.

In the Struggle

When I was experiencing a financial struggle in my life, it was if I had a disease. People seemed to distance themselves from me as if it would rub off on them. No one likes to be in a struggle. Every now and then, we may have some hard times in our life that will mean a struggle for us. Struggle is a soul-searching and humbling experience.

When you are in a struggle, family members you love so much will have a closed or a blinded eye and a deaf ear. They won't want to see your need or hear about your need or lack. They grow quiet and don't want to speak or call; if they do call, they call with a problem so that you won't ask them for anything.

Friends you respect and love start to distance themselves. They stop phoning, and when you see them, they are in a hurry with no place to go, or they look past you as if they don't see you. They say, "Call me if you need anything," but when you call them, they don't answer the phone.

When you are in the struggle, it's very uncomfortable. You begin to look for someone to give you an encouraging word if they can't give anything else. When you are in a struggle, people are afraid to give even a word. Even while I was in the struggle, I was still trying to help people by speaking into their lives, when I needed someone to speak into mine.

When all else fails, at last you begin to search your own heart and soul. I sat down one day and began to look at my life. Here I had married a man who loved God and knew how to love me the way I wanted to be loved. He was everything that I was looking for in a man. Yes, we had a blended family. He made the blend mix smoothly, being the strong head of our household, which set our home in order. There is nothing like having a home out of order, with no one knowing their place. We had a balance.

Oh, we were so full of dreams. We shared the same passion of how we wanted to help the less privileged and to look into the eyes of people with real needs and help them pay off their mortgage or bring their rent up to date, to buy groceries for a family who had no food to eat, and to see the tears of joy and gratitude on their faces. We wanted not only to give to them but to speak a word into their lives that would change and make a difference so that they would be able to help someone else.

Then we both lost our jobs. I was out of work for over three years. We were still making ends meet. When my husband lost his job, we were trying to hold things together until our payout was more than our income. We started to be the family that we had dreamed of helping.

We were struggling to keep a roof over our heads, struggling to keep the cars and keep the lights and the gas on and food in our cabinets. We tried to get public assistance but were denied; then we tried to just get food stamps but were denied again.

We had borrowed a lot of money from my mother, and she would always speak an encouraging word into our lives and give me more money. I didn't want my mother to help me even though I needed it. I wanted to be the one to help her and others. Yes, other family members helped very little, and that little came with a controlling price.

We began to learn a lesson during that struggle. We knew whom to trust and discerned who was not to be trusted. We knew who loved us and cared for us. We learned how to survive. We began to speak into our own lives and be passionate. Our ears were very sensitive to hearing about opportunities and to seeing which direction to go in.

When you are in the struggle, you have a lot of time to think, and a lot of thoughts run through your mind. I began to think of all the good times we shared together and all the positive things that we wanted to do, still wanting to help people.

All I had was a pen and paper. I began to write my story in the hope that it might encourage you. When you are at the bottom, the only way now is up. Once you have been in the struggle, you are empowered and determined to make a difference in someone else's life. The struggle teaches you to focus on other people and their needs. Dare to care; think and see yourself out of the struggle, think and see yourself in abundance. Think and see yourself rich. Be and do what you think you can, and watch what happens.

Trim all the negative out of your life. Lean on the positive, and welcome that energy, and be free. I am free. We are free and living in abundance.